Dear Pollack Family,

Thank-you for having me for Shu. I am very happy Ayala is one of my close friends and in addition, I appreciate your family warmth and hospitality. I know you love to cook and make great deli rolls, so I hope you enjoy this...

Thanks again,
MIRIAM
Zain

barbecues
& salads

simple and delicious easy-to-make recipes

Lorraine Turner

p

This is a Parragon Publishing Book
First published in 2003

Parragon Publishing
Queen Street House
4 Queen Street
Bath, BA1 1HE, UK

ISBN: 1-40542-531-8

Printed in China

Produced by the Bridgewater Book Company Ltd.

Photographer Calvey Taylor Haw

Home Economist Sara Hesketh

NOTES FOR THE READER

- This book uses both imperial and metric measurements. Follow the same units of measurement throughout; do not mix imperial and metric.

- All spoon measurements are level: teaspoons are assumed to be 5 ml, and tablespoons are assumed to be 15 ml.

- Unless otherwise stated, milk is assumed to be whole milk, eggs and individual vegetables such as potatoes are medium, and pepper is freshly ground black pepper.

- Recipes using raw or very lightly cooked eggs should be avoided by infants, the elderly, pregnant women, convalescents, and anyone suffering from an illness.

- The times given are an approximate guide only. Preparation times differ according to the techniques used by different people and the cooking times may also vary from those given. Optional ingredients, variations, or serving suggestions have not been included in the calculations.

contents

introduction   4

poultry & meat   6

fish & seafood   34

vegetarian & salads   48

desserts   82

index   96

introduction

There is something wonderfully evocative about the smell of grilled food: it can conjure up memories of lazy summer evenings on the beach, or delicious aromas wafting from an outdoor campfire. Grilling al fresco has never been easier, either: there is an ever-widening range of barbecue grills available nowadays, and with the advent of portable and disposable grills, this method of cooking food has become extremely easy, cheap, and quick.

Some barbecue grills use coals or hardwood, and others are electric. Always abide by the safety instructions that come with your grill, and be careful around naked flames and fuel. Keep children and pets away from the cooking area, and position your grill so that the smoke will not be a nuisance to other people.

This book contains a delicious array of dishes, from sizzling poultry and meat and mouthwatering fish to an extravaganza of vegetarian meals and salads. To round everything off, there is also a stunning selection of quick and easy desserts. So whatever the occasion, whether you are traveling far from home or entertaining friends in your yard, there is something here to satisfy every appetite.

guide to recipe key		
	very easy	Recipes are graded as follows: 1 pea = easy; 2 peas = very easy; 3 peas = extremely easy.
	serves 4	Recipes generally serve four people. Simply halve the ingredients to serve two, taking care not to mix imperial and metric measurements.
	10 minutes	Preparation time. Where marinating, chilling, or cooling are involved, these times have been added on separately: eg, 15 minutes + 30 minutes to marinate.
	10 minutes	Cooking time. Cooking times don't include the cooking of side dishes or accompaniments served with the main dishes.

chicken satay skewers with lime
page 16

asian shrimp skewers
page 42

tabbouleh
page 74

stuffed figs
page 92

poultry
& meat

Grilling is a delicious way of cooking
a variety of different meats and poultry,
and an easy and satisfying way to prepare
meals. The poultry and meat dishes in
this chapter are all simple to prepare and
quick to cook, and the sheer variety of
accompanying ingredients and marinades
ensures that there will always be an exciting
assortment of flavorsome, mouthwatering
dishes for your barbecue grill.

spicy grilled chicken

	ingredients	
very easy	MARINADE 1½ tbsp chile oil ½ tsp brown sugar ½ tsp salt 1½ tsp allspice	4 garlic cloves, chopped 1 green chile and 1 red chile, seeded
serves 4	1½ tsp dried mixed herbs pepper	CHICKEN 4 skinless, boneless chicken breasts, cut into slices
15 minutes + 2½ hours to marinate	1½ tsp grated fresh root ginger 4 shallots, chopped 6 scallions, trimmed and finely chopped	juice of 3 limes scant ⅔ cup water wedges of fresh lime, to garnish salad greens, to serve
20–30 minutes		

Put the chile oil, sugar, salt, allspice, and mixed herbs into a food processor and season with plenty of pepper. Blend until combined.

Add the grated ginger, shallots, scallions, and garlic. Chop the chiles, add to the shallot mixture, and blend until fairly smooth. Transfer to a glass pitcher or bowl, cover with plastic wrap, and set aside.

Put the chicken slices into a nonmetallic (glass or ceramic) bowl, which will not react with acid. Pour over the lime juice and water, then add enough marinade to cover the chicken. Cover with plastic wrap and refrigerate for 2½ hours. Cover the remaining marinade with plastic wrap and refrigerate until the chicken is ready.

When the chicken slices are thoroughly marinated, lift them out and grill them over hot coals for 20–30 minutes, or until cooked right through. Turn them frequently and baste with the remaining marinade. Garnish with lime wedges and serve on a bed of salad greens.

sweet & sour chicken wings

		ingredients	
very easy	MARINADE	1 tbsp tomato paste
	2 tbsp sweet sherry	2 garlic cloves, finely chopped
serves 4	3 tbsp sherry vinegar or red wine vinegar	1 red chile, seeded and finely chopped
	4 tbsp soy sauce	CHICKEN
5 minutes + 2½ hours to marinate	generous ¾ cup orange juice	4 lb/1.8 kg chicken wings
	scant ½ cup chicken bouillon or vegetable bouillon	GARNISH
	¼ cup brown sugar	wedges of orange
20 minutes	pepper	1 long, red chile, made into a flower (see below)

Put the sherry, vinegar, soy sauce, orange juice, bouillon, and sugar into a food processor and season well. Blend until combined. Add the tomato paste, garlic, and chile, and blend until smooth. Separate the chicken wings at the joints and put them into a nonmetallic (glass or ceramic) bowl, which will not react with acid. Pour over enough marinade to cover the chicken, cover with plastic wrap and refrigerate for 2½ hours. Cover the remaining marinade with plastic wrap and refrigerate until the chicken is ready.

When the chicken wings are thoroughly marinated, lift them out and grill them over hot coals for about 20 minutes, turning them frequently and basting with the remaining marinade. Cut into a thick part of a wing to check that the chicken is cooked all the way through. If it is still pink in the middle, continue to grill until the chicken is thoroughly cooked. Garnish with orange wedges and a chile flower (made by making ½-inch/1-cm slits in a chile and soaking in iced water for 30 minutes until fanned out.)

thai-style chicken chunks

very easy	
serves 4	
10 minutes + 2½ hours to marinate	
20 minutes	

ingredients

MARINADE
1 red chile and 1 green chile, seeded
   and finely chopped
2 garlic cloves, chopped
1¾ oz/50 g chopped fresh cilantro
1 tbsp finely chopped fresh
   lemongrass
½ tsp ground turmeric
½ tsp garam masala
2 tsp brown sugar

2 tbsp fish sauce
1 tbsp lime juice
salt and pepper

CHICKEN
4 skinless, boneless chicken breasts,
   cut into small chunks

chopped fresh cilantro, to garnish

freshly cooked jasmine rice, to serve

Put the red and green chiles, garlic, cilantro, and lemongrass into a food processor and process until coarsely chopped. Add the turmeric, garam masala, sugar, fish sauce, and lime juice, season with salt and pepper, and blend until smooth.

Put the chicken chunks into a nonmetallic (glass or ceramic) bowl, which will not react with acid. Pour over enough marinade to cover the chicken, then cover with plastic wrap and refrigerate for at least 2½ hours. Cover the remaining marinade with plastic wrap and refrigerate until the chicken is ready.

When the chicken chunks are thoroughly marinated, lift them out and grill them over hot coals for 20 minutes or until cooked right through, turning them frequently and basting with the remaining marinade. Arrange the chicken on serving plates with some freshly cooked jasmine rice, garnish with chopped cilantro, and serve.

sherried chicken
& mushroom kabobs

		ingredients	
very easy		MARINADE	KABOBS
		scant ¼ cup soy sauce	6 skinless, boneless chicken
serves 4		2 tbsp sweet sherry	breasts, cubed
		scant ¼ cup vegetable oil	16 white mushrooms
		1 tsp brown sugar	16 pearl onions
15 minutes + 2½ hours to marinate		1 tbsp honey	16 cherry tomatoes
		1 garlic clove, finely chopped	fresh flatleaf parsley, to garnish
		pepper	
15–20 minutes			freshly steamed or boiled rice, to serve

Put the soy sauce, sweet sherry, oil, sugar, and honey into a large bowl. Add the garlic and mix until well combined. Season with plenty of pepper.

Thread the chicken cubes onto 8 skewers, alternating them with the mushrooms, onions, and cherry tomatoes. When the skewers are full (leave a small space at either end), transfer them to the bowl and turn them in the sherry mixture until they are well coated. Cover with plastic wrap and place in the refrigerator to marinate for at least 2½ hours.

When the kabobs are thoroughly marinated, lift them out and grill them over hot coals for 15–20 minutes or until cooked right through, turning them frequently and basting with the remaining marinade. Arrange the kabobs on a bed of freshly cooked rice, garnish with fresh flatleaf parsley, and serve.

chicken satay skewers with lime

		ingredients	
extremely easy		MARINADE	SKEWERS
		scant ½ cup soy sauce	6 skinless, boneless chicken
serves 4		scant ½ cup lime juice	breasts, cubed
		2 tbsp smooth peanut butter	
		2 tbsp garam masala	GARNISH
10 minutes + 2½ hours to marinate		1 tbsp brown sugar	fresh cilantro leaves, shredded
		2 garlic cloves, finely chopped	wedges of lime
		1 small red chile, seeded and	
		finely chopped	freshly steamed or boiled rice, or crisp
15 minutes		pepper	salad greens, to serve

Put the soy sauce, lime juice, peanut butter, garam masala, sugar, garlic, and chile into a large bowl and mix until well combined. Season with plenty of pepper.

Thread the chicken cubes onto skewers (leave a small space at either end). Transfer them to the bowl and turn them in the peanut butter mixture until they are well coated. Cover with plastic wrap and place in the refrigerator to marinate for at least 2½ hours.

When the skewers are thoroughly marinated, lift them out and grill them over hot coals for 15 minutes or until cooked right through, turning them frequently and basting with the remaining marinade. Arrange the skewers on a bed of freshly cooked rice or crisp salad greens, garnish with cilantro leaves and lime wedges, and serve.

tangy pork ribs

easy	
serves 4	
15 minutes	
2½–2¾ hours	

ingredients

1¼ tsp salt	1 tbsp chopped flatleaf parsley
2 tsp paprika	1 tbsp sweet sherry
2 tsp pepper	1½ tbsp brown sugar
3 lb/1.3 kg pork ribs	4 tbsp Chinese chile bean sauce
1 tbsp chile or vegetable oil	1 tbsp tomato paste
1 onion, finely chopped	1 tbsp rice wine
6 scallions, trimmed and chopped	1 tbsp sherry vinegar
3 garlic cloves, chopped	scant ½ cup orange juice
2 tsp finely chopped fresh ginger root	2½ tbsp soy sauce
1 red chile, chopped	salt and pepper
1 tbsp chopped fresh cilantro	wedges of orange, to serve

Preheat the oven to 475°F/240°C. Combine the salt, paprika, and pepper in a baking dish and then add the ribs. Turn them in the dish to coat them well all over. Cook in the center of the preheated oven for 1¾–2 hours, then remove the dish from the oven, lift out the ribs, drain off the fat, and set aside.

Heat the oil in a skillet. Add the onion, scallions, garlic, ginger, and chile, and stir-fry over a high heat for 1 minute. Then add the herbs, sherry, sugar, chile bean sauce, tomato paste, rice wine, vinegar, orange juice, and soy sauce. Stir in a large pinch of salt and season well with pepper. Bring to a boil, lower the heat, and simmer for 15–20 minutes, stirring occasionally.

To cook the ribs, coat them in the sauce, then grill them over hot coals for 7–10 minutes on each side, or until cooked right through, turning them frequently and basting with more sauce as necessary. Serve at once, accompanied by orange wedges.

curried lamb skewers

		ingredients	
very easy	MARINADE	1 red or green bell pepper, seeded and
	2 tsp vegetable oil	cut into small chunks
	1 tsp curry powder	2 zucchini, cubed
serves 4	1 tsp garam masala	16 pearl onions
	2 tsp granulated sugar	
	generous ¾ cup plain yogurt	fresh cilantro leaves, to garnish
20 minutes		
+ 8 hours	SKEWERS	TO SERVE
to marinate	14 oz/400 g boneless lamb, cubed	freshly steamed or boiled rice
	5 oz/140 g dried apricot halves	crisp salad greens
15 minutes		

Put the oil, spices, sugar, and yogurt into a large bowl and mix until well combined.

Thread the lamb onto 8 skewers, alternating it with the apricot halves, red or green bell pepper, zucchini, and onions. When the skewers are full (leave a small space at either end), transfer them to the bowl and turn them in the yogurt mixture until they are well coated. Cover with plastic wrap and place in the refrigerator to marinate for at least 8 hours or overnight.

When the skewers are thoroughly marinated, lift them out and grill them over hot coals, turning them frequently, for 15 minutes or until the meat is cooked right through. Serve with freshly cooked rice and crisp salad greens, garnished with fresh cilantro leaves.

thai-spiced beef
& bell pepper kabobs

very easy	
serves 4	
20 minutes + 2½ hours to marinate	
10–15 minutes	

ingredients

MARINADE
2 tbsp sherry
2 tbsp rice wine
scant ⅓ cup soy sauce
scant ⅓ cup hoisin sauce
3 cloves garlic, finely chopped
1 red chile, seeded and
  finely chopped
1½ tbsp grated fresh root ginger

3 scallions, trimmed and finely
  chopped
salt and pepper

KABOBS
2 lb 4 oz/1 kg loin end or short loin
  steak, cubed
2 large red bell peppers, seeded and
  cut into small chunks

green and red lettuce, to serve

Put the sherry, rice wine, soy sauce, hoisin sauce, garlic, chile, ginger, and scallions into a large bowl and mix until well combined. Season to taste.

Thread the meat onto 8 skewers, alternating it with chunks of red bell pepper. When the skewers are full (leave a small space at either end), transfer them to the bowl and turn them in the soy sauce mixture until they are well coated. Cover with plastic wrap and place in the refrigerator to marinate for 2½ hours or overnight.

When the skewers are thoroughly marinated, lift them out and grill them over hot coals, turning them frequently, for 10–15 minutes or until the meat is cooked right through. Serve at once on a bed of green and red lettuce.

greek-style beef kabobs

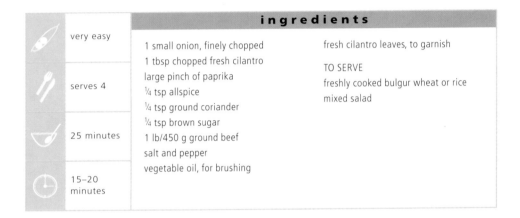

		ingredients	
very easy	1 small onion, finely chopped	fresh cilantro leaves, to garnish	
	1 tbsp chopped fresh cilantro		
	large pinch of paprika	TO SERVE	
serves 4	¼ tsp allspice	freshly cooked bulgur wheat or rice	
	¼ tsp ground coriander	mixed salad	
	¼ tsp brown sugar		
25 minutes	1 lb/450 g ground beef		
	salt and pepper		
	vegetable oil, for brushing		
15–20 minutes			

Put the onion, fresh cilantro, spices, sugar, and beef into a large bowl and mix until well combined.

On a clean counter, use your hands to shape the mixture into sausages around skewers. Brush them lightly with vegetable oil.

Grill the kabobs over hot coals, turning them frequently, for 15–20 minutes or until cooked right through. Arrange the kabobs on a platter of freshly cooked bulgur wheat or rice and garnish with fresh cilantro leaves. Serve with a mixed salad.

cherry tomato, ham
& pineapple skewers

		ingredients	
	extremely easy	1 tbsp vegetable oil 1 tbsp white wine vinegar 1 tsp mustard powder 1 tbsp honey 1 lb/450 g cooked ham steak, cubed 1 lb/450 g canned pineapple chunks, drained 12 cherry tomatoes	freshly cooked rice, fresh salad greens, or crusty bread, to serve
	serves 4		
	10 minutes		
	10 minutes		

Put the oil, vinegar, mustard powder, and honey into a bowl and mix until well combined.

Thread the ham onto skewers, alternating it with pineapple chunks and whole cherry tomatoes. When the skewers are full (leave a small space at either end), brush them with the honey mixture until they are well coated.

Grill the skewers over hot coals, turning them frequently, for about 10 minutes or until cooked right through. Serve them with freshly boiled rice, fresh salad greens, or crusty bread.

grilled pork sausages
with thyme

very easy	
serves 4	
15 minutes + 45 minutes to chill	
15 minutes	

ingredients

1 garlic clove, finely chopped
1 onion, grated
1 small red chile, seeded and
    finely chopped
1 lb/450 g lean ground pork
⅓ cup almonds, toasted
    and ground
1 cup fresh bread crumbs
1 tbsp finely chopped fresh thyme
salt and pepper

flour, for dusting
vegetable oil, for brushing

TO SERVE
fresh bread rolls
slices of onion, lightly cooked
tomato catsup and/or mustard

Put the garlic, onion, chile, pork, almonds, bread crumbs, and fresh thyme into a large bowl. Season well with salt and pepper and mix until well combined.

Using your hands, form the mixture into sausage shapes. Roll each sausage in a little flour, then transfer to a bowl, cover with plastic wrap, and refrigerate for 45 minutes.

Brush a piece of aluminum foil with oil, then put the sausages on the foil and brush them with a little more vegetable oil. Transfer the sausages and foil to the barbecue grill. Grill over hot coals, turning the sausages frequently, for about 15 minutes or until cooked right through. Serve with bread rolls, cooked sliced onion, and tomato catsup and/or mustard.

spicy thai-style burgers

		ingredients	
very easy		scant ½ cup fresh bread crumbs, white or whole-wheat 1½ tbsp finely chopped scallions 1 garlic clove, finely chopped 1½ tbsp chopped fresh lemongrass 1½ tbsp chopped fresh cilantro ½ oz/15 g almonds, chopped ½ oz/15 g groundnuts, chopped 1 lb 2 oz/500 g ground beef	1 small red chile, seeded and finely chopped salt and pepper TO SERVE wedges of lemon and lime fresh shredded Napa cabbage hamburger buns
serves 4			
15 minutes			
10–16 minutes			

Put the bread crumbs, scallions, garlic, lemongrass, cilantro, nuts, beef, and chile into a large bowl, and mix until well combined. Season with salt and pepper.

Using your hands, form the mixture into burger shapes. Grill the burgers over hot coals for 5–8 minutes on each side or until cooked right through. Serve in hamburger buns with wedges of lemon and lime, and shredded Napa cabbage.

beefburgers with chile & basil

		ingredients	
very easy		1 lb 7 oz/650 g ground beef	sprigs of fresh basil, to garnish
		1 red bell pepper, seeded and	hamburger buns, to serve
serves 4		finely chopped	
		1 garlic clove, finely chopped	
		2 small red chiles, seeded and	
10 minutes		finely chopped	
		1 tbsp chopped fresh basil	
		½ tsp powdered cumin	
10–16 minutes		salt and pepper	

Put the ground beef, red bell pepper, garlic, chiles, chopped basil, and cumin into a bowl and mix until well combined. Season with salt and pepper.

Using your hands, form the mixture into burger shapes. Grill the burgers over hot coals for 5–8 minutes on each side or until cooked right through. Garnish with sprigs of basil and serve with hamburger buns.

fish & seafood

Fish is a very healthy food: it is rich in vitamins and minerals, and offers a nutritious alternative to poultry and meat. This chapter contains some delicious recipes that you can easily prepare and cook on a barbecue grill. It rings the changes with a variety of fresh fish including tuna, salmon, and John Dory, and a wealth of accompanying ingredients and flavors from different parts of the world.

grilled salmon

		ingredients	
	extremely easy	**MARINADE** scant ½ cup vegetable oil scant ½ cup dry white wine 1 tbsp black molasses 1 tbsp brown sugar 1 tbsp soy sauce 1 garlic clove, chopped pinch of allspice salt and pepper	**SALMON** 4 salmon steaks, about 7 oz/200 g each wedges of lemon, to garnish crisp salad greens, to serve
	serves 4		
	5 minutes + 2 hours to marinate		
	20 minutes		

Put the oil, wine, black molasses, sugar, soy sauce, garlic, and allspice into a large bowl, and mix until well combined. Season with salt and pepper.

Rinse the salmon steaks under cold running water, then pat dry with paper towels. Add them to the wine mixture and turn them until they are well coated. Cover with plastic wrap and place in the refrigerator to marinate for at least 2 hours or overnight.

When the steaks are thoroughly marinated, lift them out and grill them over hot coals for about 10 minutes on each side or until cooked right through, turning them frequently and basting with the remaining marinade. About halfway through the cooking time, add the lemon wedges and cook for 4–5 minutes, turning once. Arrange the steaks on a bed of fresh salad greens, garnish with the lemon wedges, and serve.

spicy john dory

		ingredients	
very easy		AIOLI	2 garlic cloves, chopped
		4 large garlic cloves, finely chopped	2 shallots, grated
serves 4		2 small egg yolks	1 small red chile, seeded and chopped
		scant 1 cup extra-virgin olive oil	1 tbsp lemon juice
		2 tbsp lemon juice	
15 minutes		1 tbsp Dijon mustard	wedges of lemon, to garnish
		1 tbsp chopped fresh tarragon	
		salt and pepper	TO SERVE
			crisp salad greens
15 minutes		JOHN DORY	raw and lightly blanched vegetables
		2 John Dory, filleted	

To make the aioli, put the garlic and egg yolks into a food processor and process until well blended. With the motor running, slowly pour in the olive oil through the feeder tube until a thick mayonnaise forms. Add the lemon juice, mustard, tarragon, and seasoning, and blend until smooth. Transfer to a nonmetallic (glass or ceramic) bowl, which will not react with acid. Cover with plastic wrap and refrigerate until ready to serve.

Rinse the fish under cold running water, then pat dry with paper towels. In a separate bowl, mix together the garlic, shallots, chile, and lemon juice. Rub the shallot mixture onto both sides of the fillets, then grill them over hot coals for about 15 minutes or until cooked right through, turning them once. Arrange the steaks on a bed of crisp salad greens, garnish with lemon wedges, and serve separately with the aioli and the vegetables for dipping.

tuna & tarragon skewers

		ingredients	
	extremely easy	**MARINADE** 2 tbsp white wine 3 tbsp balsamic vinegar 1 tbsp extra-virgin olive oil 1 garlic clove, finely chopped salt and pepper	chopped fresh tarragon, to garnish **TO SERVE** freshly cooked rice mixed salad
	serves 4		
	10 minutes + 30 minutes to marinate	**SKEWERS** 10½ oz/300 g fresh tuna steaks 1 lb/450 g white mushrooms	
	10 minutes		

Put the wine, vinegar, olive oil, and garlic into a large bowl, and mix until well combined. Season with salt and pepper to taste.

Rinse the tuna steaks under cold running water and pat dry with paper towels. Cut them into small cubes. Wipe the mushrooms clean with paper towels. Thread the tuna cubes onto skewers, alternating them with the mushrooms. When the skewers are full (leave a small space at either end), transfer them to the bowl and turn them in the wine mixture until they are well coated. Cover with plastic wrap and place in the refrigerator to marinate for at least 30 minutes.

Grill the skewers over hot coals for about 10 minutes or until the tuna is cooked right through (but do not overcook), turning them frequently and basting with the remaining marinade. Arrange the skewers on a bed of rice, garnish with chopped fresh tarragon, and serve with a mixed salad.

asian shrimp skewers

very easy	**ingredients**	

serves 4	**MARINADE**
	scant ½ cup vegetable oil
	2 tbsp chile oil
	scant ¼ cup lemon juice
	1 tbsp rice wine or sherry
	2 scallions, trimmed and
	  finely chopped
	2 garlic cloves, finely chopped
	1 tbsp grated fresh root ginger
	1 tbsp chopped fresh lemongrass
		2 tbsp chopped fresh cilantro
		salt and pepper
		
		SKEWERS
		2 lb 4 oz/1 kg jumbo shrimp, peeled
		  and deveined, but with tails left on
		
		GARNISH
		wedges of lemon
		chopped fresh chives
		
		freshly cooked jasmine rice, to serve

15 minutes + 2 hours to marinate		
4–5 minutes		

Put the oils, lemon juice, rice wine, scallions, garlic, ginger, lemongrass, and cilantro into a food processor and season well with salt and pepper. Process until smooth, then transfer to a nonmetallic (glass or ceramic) bowl, which will not react with acid.

Add the shrimp to the bowl and turn them in the mixture until they are well coated. Cover with plastic wrap and place in the refrigerator to marinate for at least 2 hours.

When the shrimp are thoroughly marinated, lift them out and thread them onto skewers leaving a small space at either end. Grill them over hot coals for 4–5 minutes or until cooked right through (but do not overcook), turning them frequently and basting with the remaining marinade. Arrange the skewers on a bed of freshly cooked jasmine rice, garnish with lemon wedges and chopped fresh chives, and serve.

shrimp & bell pepper kabobs

very easy	
serves 4	
15 minutes + 3–4 hours to marinate	
4–5 minutes	

ingredients

MARINADE
2 scallions, trimmed and chopped
2 garlic cloves, finely chopped
1 green chile and 1 small red chile, seeded and finely chopped
1 tbsp grated fresh root ginger
1 tbsp chopped fresh chives
4 tbsp lime juice
1 tbsp finely grated lime zest
2 tbsp chile oil
salt and pepper

KABOBS
24 jumbo shrimp, peeled and deveined, but with tails left on
2 bell peppers, 1 red and 1 green, seeded and cut into small chunks

GARNISH
wedges of lime

freshly cooked rice or Napa cabbage, to serve

Put the scallions, garlic, chiles, ginger, chives, lime juice, lime zest, and chile oil into a food processor and season well with salt and pepper. Process until smooth, then transfer to a nonmetallic (glass or ceramic) bowl, which will not react with acid.

Thread the shrimp onto skewers, alternating them with the red and green bell pepper chunks. When the skewers are full (leave a small space at either end), transfer them to the bowl and turn them in the mixture until they are well coated. Cover with plastic wrap and place in the refrigerator to marinate for 3–4 hours.

Grill the kabobs over hot coals for 4–5 minutes or until the shrimp are cooked right through (but do not overcook), turning them frequently and basting with the remaining marinade. Arrange the skewers on a bed of rice or Napa cabbage, garnish with lime wedges and chopped fresh chives, and serve.

sweet & sour polynesian shrimp

extremely easy	
serves 4	
5 minutes	
8–10 minutes	

ingredients

SAUCE
10½ oz/300 g canned pineapple
   chunks
scant ¼ cup soy sauce
2 tbsp sweet sherry
3 tbsp red wine vinegar
¼ cup brown sugar

KABOBS
6 strips smoked lean bacon
8 oz/225 g jumbo shrimp, peeled and
   deveined, tails removed
2 bell peppers, 1 red and 1 orange,
   seeded and cut into small chunks

freshly boiled rice, to serve

To make the sauce, drain the pineapple chunks and reserve the juice. Set the pineapple chunks aside for the kabobs. In a separate large bowl, mix together the soy sauce, sherry, red wine vinegar, and sugar, then stir in the reserved pineapple juice.

For the kabobs, cut the bacon strips into small pieces and wrap a piece around each shrimp. Thread the shrimp onto skewers, alternating them with pieces of red and orange bell pepper and the reserved pineapple chunks. When the skewers are full (leave a small space at either end), transfer them to the large bowl and turn them in the mixture until they are well coated.

Grill the kabobs over hot coals for 8–10 minutes or until the shrimp are cooked right through (but do not overcook), turning them frequently and brushing with more sauce as necessary. Arrange the kabobs on a bed of freshly cooked rice and serve.

vegetarian & salads

Vegetarian cooking has really come into its own in recent years, and what better way to celebrate its versatility and diversity than on the barbecue grill? There has never been a better time for experimenting with new ingredients and combinations, especially with the ever-widening range of delicious vegetables and fruits now available to us. This chapter provides some mouthwatering vegetarian dishes to tempt your palate, and an exciting selection of salads which make wonderful accompaniments or light meals in themselves.

mycoprotein & mushroom skewers

		ingredients
very easy	MARINADE 2 tbsp extra-virgin olive oil	1 lb/450 g white mushrooms 1 large pear, cored and cut into
	1 tbsp balsamic vinegar	small chunks
serves 4	1 garlic clove, finely chopped	
	salt and pepper	wedges of pear, to garnish
10 minutes + 1 hour to marinate	SKEWERS 1 lb 10 oz/750 g mycoprotein pieces,	TO SERVE fresh green and red lettuce fresh crusty bread
	or mycoprotein fillets cut into	
5 minutes	small chunks	

Put the oil, vinegar, and garlic into a large bowl. Season with salt and pepper and mix until well combined.

Thread the mycoprotein pieces onto skewers, alternating them with the mushrooms and pear chunks. When the skewers are full (leave a small space at either end), transfer them to the bowl and turn them in the mixture until they are well coated. Cover with plastic wrap and place in the refrigerator to marinate for at least 1 hour.

Grill the skewers over hot coals for about 5 minutes or until the mycoprotein is cooked right through, turning them frequently and basting with the remaining marinade. Arrange the skewers on a bed of fresh green and red lettuce, garnish with wedges of pear, and serve with fresh crusty bread.

bean & vegetable burgers
with tomato salsa

		ingredients	
very easy		**BURGERS**	**SALSA**
		7 oz/200 g canned garbanzo beans, drained and rinsed	4 large tomatoes, chopped
serves 4		7 oz/200 g canned cannellini beans, drained and rinsed	1 tbsp lime juice
			2 shallots, peeled and chopped
		1 large zucchini, finely grated	1 garlic clove, peeled and chopped
15 minutes + 30 minutes to chill		1 large carrot, peeled and finely grated	1 tbsp chopped fresh basil
		1 garlic clove, peeled and finely chopped	**GARNISH**
		3 oz/75 g bread crumbs	chopped fresh basil
10–20 minutes		salt and pepper	wedges of lime
			hamburger buns, to serve

Put the garbanzo beans and cannellini beans into a food processor and blend together briefly. Transfer to a large bowl, then add the zucchini, carrot, garlic, and bread crumbs. Season with salt and pepper, then mix together until thoroughly combined. Using your hands, form the mixture into burger shapes, transfer to a shallow dish, and cover with plastic wrap. Refrigerate for 30 minutes.

To make the salsa, put the tomatoes, lime juice, shallots, garlic, and basil into a bowl and stir together. Cover with plastic wrap and set aside.

Grill the burgers over hot coals for 5–10 minutes on each side or until cooked right through. Remove from the coals and transfer to serving plates. Garnish with chopped basil and wedges of lime and serve with hamburger buns and the salsa.

mixed nut burgers with chile

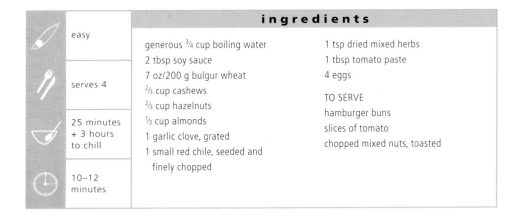

	ingredients	
easy	generous ¾ cup boiling water	1 tsp dried mixed herbs
	2 tbsp soy sauce	1 tbsp tomato paste
serves 4	7 oz/200 g bulgur wheat	4 eggs
	⅔ cup cashews	
	⅔ cup hazelnuts	TO SERVE
25 minutes + 3 hours to chill	⅓ cup almonds	hamburger buns
	1 garlic clove, grated	slices of tomato
	1 small red chile, seeded and finely chopped	chopped mixed nuts, toasted
10–12 minutes		

Pour the boiling water and soy sauce into a heatproof bowl. Rinse and drain the bulgur wheat three times, then add it to the bowl and stir into the liquid. Let stand for 15–20 minutes, or until all the liquid has been absorbed.

While the bulgur wheat is soaking, grind the cashews, hazelnuts, and almonds in a food processor. When the bulgur wheat is ready (and all the liquid has been absorbed), add the ground nuts to the bowl and stir them in. Then add the garlic, chile, mixed herbs, tomato paste, and eggs, and mix until well combined. Cover with plastic wrap and refrigerate for 3 hours.

When the mixture has chilled, form it into burger shapes, then grill over hot coals for 10–12 minutes or until cooked through, turning once. About halfway through the cooking time, add the tomato slices. Cook for 4–5 minutes, turning once. Serve at once with hamburger buns, the tomato slices, and toasted chopped nuts.

stuffed tortillas

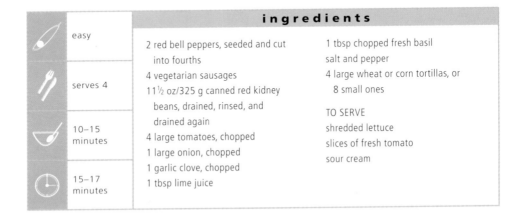

		ingredients	
easy		2 red bell peppers, seeded and cut into fourths	1 tbsp chopped fresh basil
			salt and pepper
serves 4		4 vegetarian sausages	4 large wheat or corn tortillas, or
		11½ oz/325 g canned red kidney beans, drained, rinsed, and drained again	8 small ones
10–15 minutes		4 large tomatoes, chopped	TO SERVE
		1 large onion, chopped	shredded lettuce
		1 garlic clove, chopped	slices of fresh tomato
15–17 minutes		1 tbsp lime juice	sour cream

Cook the red bell peppers on the barbecue grill, skin side down, for about 5 minutes or until the skins are blackened and charred. Transfer them to a plastic bag, seal the bag, and set aside.

Grill the sausages over hot coals for 10–12 minutes or until cooked right through, turning them occasionally. While the sausages are cooking, put the kidney beans, tomatoes, onion, garlic, lime juice, and basil into a large bowl. Season with salt and pepper and mix until well combined.

Take the bell pepper pieces from the plastic bag and remove the skins. Chop the flesh into small pieces and add it to the kidney bean mixture. About one minute before the sausages are ready, warm the tortillas on the grill for a few seconds.

Remove the sausages from the grill and cut them into slices. Fill the tortillas with sausage slices, kidney bean salsa, shredded lettuce, tomato slices, and sour cream. Serve at once.

haloumi cheese
& vegetable kabobs

		ingredients	
	very easy	**MARINADE** 4 tbsp extra-virgin olive oil 2 tbsp balsamic vinegar 2 garlic cloves, finely chopped 1 tbsp chopped fresh cilantro salt and pepper	12 cherry tomatoes 2 zucchini, cut into small chunks 1 red bell pepper, seeded and cut into small chunks chopped fresh cilantro, to garnish
	serves 4		
	10 minutes + 2 hours to marinate	**KABOBS** 8 oz/225 g haloumi cheese 12 white mushrooms 8 pearl onions	**TO SERVE** freshly cooked rice or fresh salad greens fresh crusty bread
	5–10 minutes		

Put the oil, vinegar, garlic, and cilantro into a large bowl. Season with salt and pepper and mix until well combined.

Cut the haloumi cheese into bite-size cubes. Thread the cubes onto skewers, alternating them with whole white mushrooms, pearl onions, cherry tomatoes, and zucchini and red bell pepper chunks. When the skewers are full (leave a small space at either end), transfer them to the bowl and turn them in the mixture until they are well coated. Cover with plastic wrap and place in the refrigerator to marinate for at least 2 hours.

When the skewers are thoroughly marinated, grill them over hot coals for 5–10 minutes or until they are cooked to your taste, turning them frequently and basting with the remaining marinade. Arrange the skewers on a bed of freshly cooked rice or fresh mixed salad greens, garnish with cilantro leaves, and serve with fresh crusty bread.

chile beanburgers
with onion salsa

easy	
serves 4	
15–20 minutes	
10–20 minutes	

ingredients

SALSA
4 large tomatoes, chopped
1 red onion, finely chopped
1 garlic clove, chopped
1 tbsp chopped fresh cilantro
1 tbsp chopped fresh flatleaf parsley
1 tbsp red wine vinegar
1 tbsp lime juice
salt and pepper

BURGERS
8 oz/225 g canned red kidney beans
1 large carrot, boiled and mashed
1 large red onion, finely chopped
½ cup fresh bread crumbs
4 tbsp all-purpose flour
1 tbsp tomato paste
sprigs of fresh cilantro and wedges of
   lime, to garnish
hamburger buns and vegetarian cheese
   slices, to serve

To make the salsa, put the tomatoes, onion, garlic, herbs, vinegar, and lime juice into a bowl. Season with salt and pepper and mix until well combined. Cover with plastic wrap and set aside.

To make the burgers, drain the canned kidney beans, rinse them, and drain them again. Put them into a large mixing bowl with the carrot, onion, bread crumbs, flour, and tomato paste, and mix until well combined. Season well with salt and pepper. Using your hands, form the mixture into burger shapes. Grill the burgers over hot coals for 5–10 minutes on each side or until cooked right through. Garnish with sprigs of fresh cilantro and wedges of lime, and serve with hamburger buns and cheese slices.

cheese & vegetable rolls

		ingredients	
easy	2 red bell peppers, seeded and cut into fourths	4 large white or whole-wheat rolls, cut in half horizontally to make
serves 4	2 zucchini, trimmed and sliced	8 thinner rounds
	1 large onion, cut into rings	4 oz/115 g smoked (cured) semifirm
	5½ oz/150 g baby corn	cheese, grated
15 minutes	3 tbsp olive oil	4 tbsp sour cream
10 minutes		

Cook the bell peppers on the barbecue grill, skin side down, for 5 minutes or until the skins are charred. Transfer them to a plastic bag, seal it, and set aside. Brush the zucchini, onion rings, and corn with oil, and grill over hot coals for 5 minutes, turning them frequently and basting with more oil if necessary.

While the vegetables are grilling, take the bottom halves of the bread rolls, brush the cut sides with oil, sprinkle over some cheese, and cover with the top halves. Wrap each roll in aluminum foil and transfer them to the grill. Warm for 2–4 minutes, just until the cheese starts to melt (do not overcook).

While the rolls are warming, take the bell pepper pieces from the bag and remove the skins. Chop the flesh into small pieces and transfer it to a plate with the other vegetables.

Transfer the rolls to serving plates and remove the foil. Fill them with the cooked vegetables and sour cream and serve at once.

spicy vegetarian sausages

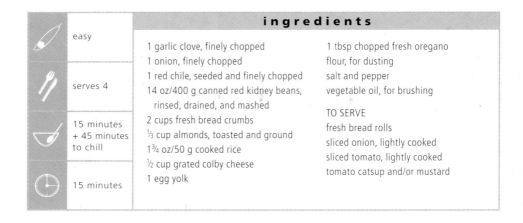

		ingredients	
easy			
serves 4	1 garlic clove, finely chopped 1 onion, finely chopped 1 red chile, seeded and finely chopped 14 oz/400 g canned red kidney beans, rinsed, drained, and mashed	1 tbsp chopped fresh oregano flour, for dusting salt and pepper vegetable oil, for brushing	
15 minutes + 45 minutes to chill	2 cups fresh bread crumbs ⅓ cup almonds, toasted and ground 1¾ oz/50 g cooked rice ½ cup grated colby cheese 1 egg yolk	TO SERVE fresh bread rolls sliced onion, lightly cooked sliced tomato, lightly cooked tomato catsup and/or mustard	
15 minutes			

Put the garlic, onion, chile, mashed kidney beans, bread crumbs, almonds, rice, and cheese into a large bowl. Stir in the egg yolk and oregano, then season with salt and plenty of pepper.

Using your hands, form the mixture into sausage shapes. Roll each sausage in a little flour, then transfer to a bowl, cover with plastic wrap, and refrigerate for 45 minutes.

Brush a piece of aluminum foil with oil, then put the sausages on the foil and brush them with a little more vegetable oil. Transfer the sausages and foil to the barbecue grill. Grill over hot coals, turning the sausages frequently, for about 15 minutes or until cooked right through. Serve with bread rolls, cooked sliced onion and tomato, and tomato catsup and/or mustard.

carrot, cabbage
& mixed fruit salad

		ingredients	
extremely easy	7 oz/200 g raw carrots	generous ⅓ cup golden raisins	
	7 oz/200 g raw white cabbage	generous ⅓ cup raisins	
serves 4	3½ oz/100 g sprouting beans	1 tbsp lemon juice	
	1¾ oz/50 g alfalfa sprouts		
10 minutes			
—			

Trim and peel the carrots, then grate them into a large salad bowl. Trim the white cabbage, then shred it finely. Transfer it to a large strainer and rinse under cold running water. Drain well, then add it to the carrots.

Put the sprouting beans and alfalfa into the strainer and rinse well, then drain and add to the salad. Rinse and drain all the fruit and then add it to the bowl. Pour in the lemon juice, toss the salad in it, and serve.

beet, apple & celery salad

		ingredients
extremely easy		2 apples
		2 large or 4 small cooked beets
serves 4		2 celery stalks
		scant ½ cup plain yogurt
5–10 minutes		1 tbsp lemon juice
—		

Wash and core the apples, but leave the skin on. Grate them into a large salad bowl.

Grate the beets, then add them to the bowl with the apples. Wash and trim the celery stalks, cut them into small pieces, then add them to the salad.

Add the yogurt and lemon juice, mix until all the ingredients are thoroughly combined, then serve.

avocado, corn & walnut salad

		ingredients
	extremely easy	12 oz/350 g canned corn kernels
		2¾ oz/75 g walnuts, chopped
		2 large, ripe avocados
	serves 4	6 tbsp lemon juice
		6 tbsp sour cream
	10 minutes	1 oz/25 g walnuts, chopped, to garnish
	—	

Drain the corn kernels, then put them into a large salad bowl. Add the walnuts and mix until well combined.

Peel and pit the avocados, brush them with some of the lemon juice to prevent discoloration, then add them to the salad.

In a separate bowl, mix the remaining lemon juice with the sour cream until a smooth consistency is reached. Add more lemon juice or cream if necessary. Add the lemon cream to the salad, stir it in, sprinkle with chopped walnuts, and serve.

fava beans with
mozzarella & basil

		ingredients	
extremely easy	1 lb/450 g fava beans (shelled weight)	GARNISH finely chopped fresh mint
serves 4	4 tbsp extra-virgin olive oil 1 tbsp lime juice 1 tbsp finely chopped fresh basil 2¼ oz/60 g firm mozzarella	wedges of lime
10 minutes		
5 minutes		

Bring a pan of water to a boil, then add the fava beans and cook for 2 minutes. Drain well and let cool.

In a separate bowl, mix together the olive oil, lime juice, and chopped basil.

When the beans are cool, transfer them to a large salad bowl. Pour over the oil dressing and mix until well combined. Cut the mozzarella into cubes and stir them gently into the salad. Garnish with chopped fresh mint and lime wedges and serve.

tabbouleh

extremely easy		
serves 4		
25 minutes		
2 minutes		

ingredients

7 oz/200 g bulgur wheat
½ cucumber
4 ripe tomatoes
3 scallions
3½ oz/100 g fresh flatleaf parsley
3½ oz/100 g fresh mint
juice of ½ lemon

chopped fresh parsley, to garnish

TO SERVE
4 pitas
wedges of lemon

Rinse and drain the bulgur wheat three times, then transfer it to a large heatproof bowl.

Bring a pot of water to a boil. Pour over enough boiling water to cover the bulgur wheat, with about ½ inch/1 cm more on top. Set aside for 15–20 minutes or until the water has been absorbed.

While the bulgur wheat is soaking, prepare the salad. Peel the cucumber, cut it into small cubes, and transfer it to a large salad bowl. Wash and chop the tomatoes and trim and chop the scallions, then add them to the bowl. Wash and chop the herbs, and add them to the salad with the lemon juice.

When the bulgur wheat is ready, squeeze out any remaining moisture and add it to the salad. Toss the ingredients together and garnish with chopped parsley. Warm the pitas on the barbecue grill for a few seconds, then pass them round with the tabbouleh so that people can stuff them with the salad. Serve with wedges of lemon.

spicy tomato salad

		ingredients	
	extremely easy	4 large ripe tomatoes 1 oz/25 g fresh basil 1 small red chile 1 garlic clove 4 tbsp extra-virgin olive oil	GARNISH sprigs of fresh basil wedges of lemon
	serves 4		fresh crusty bread, to serve
	5 minutes + 10 minutes to cool	1 tbsp lemon juice 2 tbsp balsamic vinegar salt and pepper	
	2–4 minutes		

Bring a pot of water to a boil. Put the tomatoes into a heatproof bowl, then pour over enough boiling water to cover them. Let them soak for 2–4 minutes, then lift them out of the water and let cool slightly.

When the tomatoes are cool enough to handle, gently pierce the skins with the point of a knife. You should now find the skins easy to remove. Discard the skins, then chop the tomatoes and place them in a large salad bowl.

Seed and finely chop the chile, then chop the garlic. Wash and finely chop the basil, then add it to the tomatoes with the chile and the garlic.

In a separate bowl, mix together the oil, lemon juice, and balsamic vinegar, then season with salt and pepper. Pour the mixture over the salad and toss together well. Garnish with basil sprigs and lemon wedges, and serve with fresh crusty bread.

mixed cabbage coleslaw
with fruit

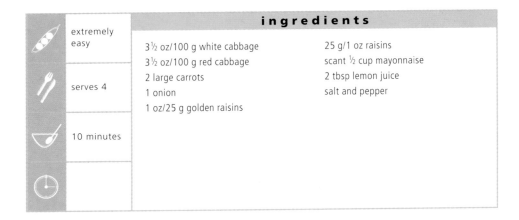

	ingredients	
extremely easy	3 ½ oz/100 g white cabbage	25 g/1 oz raisins
	3 ½ oz/100 g red cabbage	scant ½ cup mayonnaise
serves 4	2 large carrots	2 tbsp lemon juice
	1 onion	salt and pepper
10 minutes	1 oz/25 g golden raisins	

Wash and shred the white and red cabbage. Grate the carrots, and finely chop the onion. Put all the prepared vegetables into a large salad bowl, then wash the fruit and add to the bowl.

In a separate bowl, mix together the mayonnaise and lemon juice, season with salt and pepper, and pour over the salad. Mix all the ingredients together until well combined. Serve at once, or cover with plastic wrap and refrigerate until ready to use.

potato, arugula & mozzarella salad

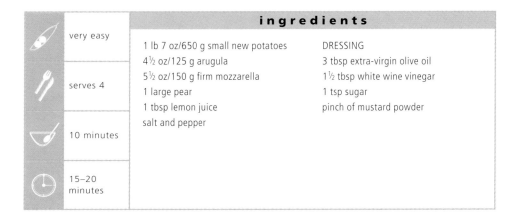

	ingredients	
very easy	1 lb 7 oz/650 g small new potatoes	DRESSING
	4½ oz/125 g arugula	3 tbsp extra-virgin olive oil
serves 4	5½ oz/150 g firm mozzarella	1½ tbsp white wine vinegar
	1 large pear	1 tsp sugar
	1 tbsp lemon juice	pinch of mustard powder
10 minutes	salt and pepper	
15–20 minutes		

Bring a pan of salted water to a boil. Add the potatoes, lower the heat, and cook for about 15 minutes, until tender. Remove from the heat, drain, and let cool.

When the potatoes are cool, cut them in half and place them in a large salad bowl. Wash and drain the arugula, cut the mozzarella into cubes, and wash, trim, and slice the pear. Add them to the bowl along with the lemon juice. Season with salt and pepper.

To make the dressing, mix together the oil, vinegar, sugar, and mustard powder. Pour the dressing over the salad and toss all the ingredients together until they are well coated. Serve at once.

desserts

Grilled desserts are a special treat and
provide a satisfying finale to any al fresco
meal. Fruits, in particular, are very healthy
and nutritious foods, and are delicious
cooked over coals. This chapter contains
some truly irresistible concoctions: some are
light and refreshing and may include
unexpected combinations, such as apple
and melon kabobs; others are rich and
indulgent, such as grilled bananas covered
with melting chocolate and a splash of rum.
All are very easy and quick to make.

apple & melon kabobs

very easy	
serves 4	
5–10 minutes	
10 minutes	

ingredients

6 tbsp butter
1–2 tbsp brown sugar
pinch of allspice
½ melon, such as galia or charentais
2 apples
1 tbsp lemon juice

plain yogurt, mascarpone cheese, or
ice cream, to serve

In a small pan, melt the butter gently over a low heat. Stir in the brown sugar and allspice, then remove from the heat and pour into a large bowl.

Cut the melon flesh into small chunks. Wash and core the apples, and cut into small chunks. Brush the fruit with lemon juice.

Thread the melon chunks onto skewers, alternating with pieces of apple. When the skewers are full (leave a small space at either end), transfer them to the bowl and turn them in the butter mixture until they are well coated.

Grill the kabobs over hot coals, turning them frequently, for about 10 minutes or until they are cooked to your taste. Serve with plain yogurt, mascarpone cheese, or ice cream.

chocolate rum bananas

		ingredients	

very easy		1 tbsp butter
		8 oz/225 g semisweet or milk
		  chocolate
		4 large bananas
		2 tbsp rum
			grated nutmeg, to decorate
			
			mascarpone cheese or ice cream,
			  to serve

serves 4			
5 minutes			
5–10 minutes			

Take four 10-inch/25-cm squares of aluminum foil and brush them with butter.

Cut the chocolate into very small pieces. Make a careful slit lengthwise in the peel of each banana, and open just wide enough to insert the chocolate. Place the chocolate pieces inside the bananas, along their lengths, then close them up.

Wrap each stuffed banana in a square of aluminum foil, then grill them over hot coals for 5–10 minutes, until the chocolate has melted inside the bananas. Remove from the barbecue grill, place the bananas on serving plates, and pour some rum into each banana. Serve at once with mascarpone cheese or ice cream topped with grated nutmeg.

brandied pineapple rings

		ingredients	
	very easy	1 pineapple, peeled, cored, and cut into rings	sprigs of fresh mint, to decorate
	serves 4	MARINADE 2 tbsp honey	
	5 minutes + 1–1½ hours to marinate	3 tbsp brandy 2 tsp lemon juice	
	10 minutes		

For the marinade, put the honey, brandy, and lemon juice into a large, nonmetallic (glass or ceramic) bowl, which will not react with acid. Stir together until well combined. Put the pineapple rings into the bowl and turn them in the mixture until thoroughly coated. Cover with plastic wrap, transfer to the refrigerator, and let marinate for 1–1½ hours.

When the pineapple rings are thoroughly marinated, lift them out and grill them over hot coals for about 10 minutes, turning them frequently and basting with more marinade if necessary.

Remove the pineapple rings from the barbecue grill, arrange them on individual serving plates, and decorate with fresh mint sprigs.

summer fruit nectarines

		ingredients
very easy	4 large nectarines 7 oz/200 g frozen summer fruits (such as blueberries and raspberries), thawed 3 tbsp lemon juice 3 tbsp honey	mascarpone cheese or ice cream, to serve
serves 4		
5 minutes		
10–15 minutes		

Cut out eight 7-inch/18-cm squares of aluminum foil. Wash the nectarines, cut them in half, and remove the pits. Place each nectarine half on a square of foil.

Fill each nectarine half with summer fruits, then top each one with 1 teaspoon of lemon juice, then 1 teaspoon of honey.

Close the foil around each nectarine half to make a package, then grill them over hot coals for 10–15 minutes, according to your taste. Remove from the barbecue grill, place the nectarines on serving plates, and serve with mascarpone cheese or ice cream.

stuffed figs

		ingredients	
easy	8 fresh figs	sprigs of fresh mint, to decorate	
serves 4	3½ oz/100 g cream cheese 1 tsp powdered cinnamon 3 tbsp brown sugar	plain yogurt, mascarpone cheese, or ice cream, to serve	
10 minutes			
10 minutes			

Cut out eight 7-inch/18-cm squares of aluminum foil. Make a small slit in each fig, then place each fig on a square of foil.

Put the cream cheese in a bowl. Add the cinnamon and stir until well combined. Stuff the inside of each fig with the cinnamon cream cheese, then sprinkle a teaspoon of sugar over each one. Close the foil round each fig to make a package.

Place the packages on the barbecue grill and cook over hot coals, turning them frequently, for about 10 minutes, or until the figs are cooked to your taste. Transfer the figs to serving plates and decorate with fresh mint. Serve at once with plain yogurt, mascarpone cheese, or ice cream.

grilled apples

		ingredients	
easy	4 apples	plain yogurt or mascarpone cheese,	
	3 tbsp lemon juice	to serve	
serves 4	3 tbsp butter		
	4 tsp brown sugar		
	8 tbsp sweet mincemeat		
10 minutes			
10 minutes			

Wash the apples, then cut them in half from top to bottom. Remove the cores and seeds, then brush the cut sides of the apples with lemon juice to prevent discoloration.

Put the butter in a small pan and gently melt it over a low heat. Remove from the heat, then brush the cut sides of the apples with half of the butter. Reserve the rest of the melted butter.

Sprinkle the apples with sugar, then transfer them to the barbecue grill, cut sides down, and cook over hot coals for about 5 minutes. Brush the apples with the remaining butter, then turn them over. Add a tablespoon of mincemeat to the center of each apple, then cook for another 5 minutes, or until they are cooked to your taste.

Remove from the heat and transfer to serving plates. Serve at once with plain yogurt or mascarpone cheese.

index

aioli 38
apples
    apple & melon kabobs 84
    beet, apple & celery
        salad 68
    grilled 94
Asian shrimp skewers 42
avocado, corn & walnut
    salad 70

bananas, chocolate rum 86
bean & vegetable burgers with
    tomato salsa 52
beanburgers with onion salsa 60
beef
    beefburgers with chile
        & basil 32
    Greek-style kabobs 24
    Thai-style burgers 30
    Thai-spiced beef & bell
        pepper kabobs 22
beet, apple, & celery salad 68
brandied pineapple rings 88
burgers
    bean & vegetable 52
    beefburgers with chile & basil
        32
    chile beanburgers 60
    mixed nut burgers with
        chile 54
    spicy Thai-style 30

carrot, cabbage & mixed fruit
    salad 66
cheese
    cheese & vegetable rolls 62
    fava beans with mozzarella
        & basil 72
    haloumi & vegetable
        kabobs 58
    potato, arugula & mozzarella
        salad 80
cherry tomato & ham skewers 26
chicken
    satay skewers with lime 16
    sherried kabobs 14
    spicy grilled 8
    sweet and sour wings 10
    Thai-style chunks 12
chile beanburgers with onion
    salsa 60
chocolate rum bananas 86
curried lamb skewers 20

fava beans with mozzarella &
    basil 72
figs, stuffed 92

fruit
    apple & melon kabobs 84
    beet, apple & celery salad 68
    brandied pineapple rings 88
    carrot, cabbage & mixed fruit
        salad 66
    chocolate rum bananas 86
    grilled apples 94
    mixed cabbage coleslaw with
        fruit 78
    stuffed figs 92
    summer fruit nectarines 90

Greek-style beef kabobs 24
grilled dishes
    apples 94
    pork sausages with thyme 28
    salmon 36

haloumi cheese & vegetable
    kabobs 58
ham, pineapple and cherry
    tomato skewers 26

John Dory, spicy 38

kabobs
    apple & melon 84
    Greek-style beef 24
    haloumi cheese
        & vegetable 58
    sherried chicken
        & mushroom 14
    shrimp & bell pepper 44
    Thai-spiced beef & bell
        pepper 22

lamb skewers 20

mycoprotein & mushroom
    skewers 50
mixed cabbage coleslaw with
    fruit 78
mixed nut burgers with chile 54
mushroom & sherried chicken
    kabobs 14

nectarines, summer fruit 90
nut burgers with chile 54

pineapple rings, brandied 88
pork
    grilled sausages with
        thyme 28
    tangy ribs 18
potato, arugula & mozzarella
    salad 80

salads
    avocado, corn & walnut 70
    beet, apple & celery 68
    carrot, cabbage & mixed
        fruit 66
    fava beans with mozzarella
        & basil 72
    mixed cabbage coleslaw with
        fruit 78
    potato, arugula
        & mozzarella 80
    spicy tomato 76
    tabbouleh 74
salmon, grilled 36
salsa
    onion 60
    tomato 52
sausages
    grilled pork with thyme 28
    spicy vegetarian 64
shrimp
    Asian skewers 42
    shrimp & bell pepper
        kabobs 44
    sweet & sour Polynesian 46
skewers
    Asian shrimp 42
    cherry tomato, pineapple &
        ham 26
    chicken satay with lime 16
    curried lamb 20
    mycoprotein & mushroom 50
    tuna & tarragon 40
spicy dishes
    grilled chicken 8
    Thai-style burgers 30
    John Dory 38
    tomato salad 76
    vegetarian sausages 64
stuffed dishes
    figs 92
    tortillas 56
summer fruit nectarines 90
sweet & sour dishes
    chicken wings 10
    Polynesian shrimp 46

tabbouleh 74
tangy pork ribs 18
Thai-style dishes
    beef & bell pepper kabobs 22
    burgers 30
    chicken chunks 12
tortillas, stuffed 56
tuna & tarragon skewers 40

vegetarian beanburgers 52
vegetarian sausages 64